Program Authors

Peter Afflerbach
Camille Blachowicz
Candy Dawson Boyd
Elena Izquierdo
Connie Juel
Edward Kame'enui
Donald Leu
Jeanne Paratore
Sam Sebesta
Deborah Simmons
Alfred Tatum
Sharon Vaughn
Susan Watts Taffe
Karen Kring Wixson

Glenview, Illinois • Boston, Massachusetts • Chandler, Arizona •
Upper Saddle River, New Jersey

We dedicate Reading Street to
Peter Jovanovich.

His wisdom, courage,
and passion for education
are an inspiration to us all.

About the Cover Artist

Rob Hefferan likes to reminisce about the simple life he had as a child growing up in Cheshire, when his biggest worry was whether to have fish fingers or Alphabetti Spaghetti for tea. The faces, colors, and shapes from that time are a present-day inspiration for his artwork.

ISBN-13: 978-0-328-47849-1
ISBN-10: 0-328-47849-0
1 2 3 4 5 6 7 8 9 10 V011 13 12 11 10 09

Dear Texas Reader,

What do you think of Reading Street so far? You've learned lots of letters and sounds and words. Have AlphaBuddy and your *My Skills Buddy* helped you along the way?

On the next part of our trip, you will read about plants and animals, and there will be a special visit to a very large beanstalk.

So hop on board, and let's get going. There's lots more to learn.

Sincerely,
The Authors

How are animals and plants unique?

Week 1

Big Book

Week 2

Week 3

Week 4

Week 5

Week 6

Reading Street The Digital Path!

Don Leu
The Internet Guy

Right before our eyes, the nature of reading and learning is changing. The Internet and other technologies create new opportunities, new solutions, and new literacies. New reading comprehension skills are required online. They are increasingly important to our students and our society.

Those of us on the Reading Street team are here to help you on this new, and very exciting, journey.

See It!

- Big Question Video
- Concept Talk Video
- Envision It! Animations
- eReaders

Hear It!

- Amazing Words *Sing With Me*
- eSelections
- Grammar Jammer

Adam and Kim play at the beach.

Get Online!
www.TexasReadingStreet.com

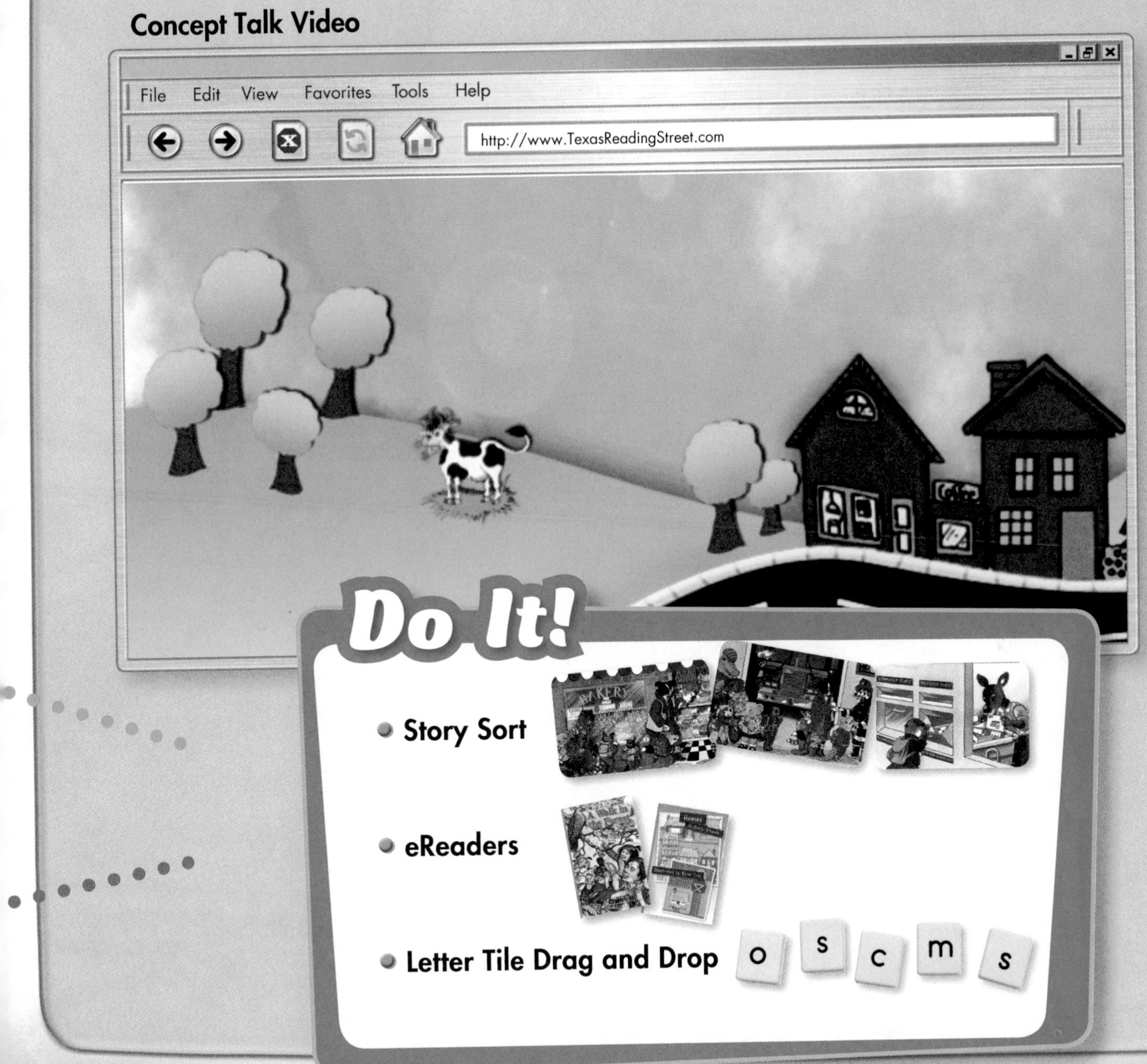
Concept Talk Video
File
Edit
View
Favorites
Tools
Help
http://www.TexasReadingStreet.com
Do It!
Story Sort
eReaders
Letter Tile Drag and Drop
o
s
c
m
s

Unit 2

Look at Us!

www.TexasReadingStreet.com
- Big Question Video
- eSelections
- Envision It! Animations
- Story Sort

How are animals and plants unique?

B

TEKS
K.2.C.1 Orally generate rhymes in response to spoken words. **K.2.E.1** Recognize spoken alliteration or groups of words that begin with the same spoken onset or initial sound. **K.2.H.1** Isolate the initial sound in spoken one-syllable words.

Phonemic Awareness

Let's Listen for

Initial Sounds

Read Together

- Say *Ann, Al, Andy.* What sound do you hear at the beginning of these names?
- Find three things that begin with /a/, like *Ann.*
- Point to these pictures and say these words: *bed, pillow, rug.* Do they begin with the same sound? What about *ant, alligator, astronaut?*
- What rhymes with *Ann?*

READING STREET ONLINE
BIG QUESTION VIDEO
www.TexasReadingStreet.com

TEKS

★Tell how facts, ideas, characters, settings, or events are the same and/or different.

Comprehension

Envision It!

Compare and Contrast

READING STREET ONLINE
PICTURE IT! ANIMATION
www.TexasReadingStreet.com

TEKS
K.3.B Use knowledge of letter-sound relationships to decode regular words in text. **K.3.D** Identify and read at least 25 high-frequency words from a commonly used list.

Envision It! | Sounds to Know

Aa

astronaut

READING STREET ONLINE
ALPHABET CARDS
www.TexasReadingStreet.com

Phonics

Short *Aa*

Words I Can Blend

High-Frequency Words

Words I Can Read

have

is

Sentences I Can Read

1. I have a mat.
2. The mat is little.
3. Tam is little.

0.TEKS

K.3.A.1 Identify the common sounds that letters represent. **K.3.B.1** Use knowledge of letter-sound relationships to decode regular words in text. **K.3.D** Identify and read at least 25 high-frequency words from a commonly used list.

Phonics

I Can Read!

Decodable Reader

- Short *a*
  am
  Tam
  mat
  at
- High-Frequency Words
  I
  am
  is
  little
  have
  a
  the
- Read the story.

READING STREET ONLINE
DECODABLE eBOOKS
www.TexasReadingStreet.com

Decodable Reader 7

A Little Mat

Written by Alex Altman
Illustrated by Mary Stern

I am Tam.

Is Tam little?

Tam is little.

I have a mat.

Is the mat little?

The mat is little.

Tam is at the mat.

TEKS
K.10.B.1 Retell important facts in a text, heard or read. ★Tell how facts, ideas, characters, settings, or events are the same and/or different.

Envision It! Retell

Big Book

READING STREET ONLINE
RETELL
www.TexasReadingStreet.com

Think, Talk, and Write

1. Tell about a unique flower you have seen. **Text to Self**

2. How are a rose and cauliflower alike? How are they different?

Compare and Contrast

3. Look back and write.

TEKS
K.5.C Identify and sort pictures of objects into conceptual categories.
K.21.A.2 Listen attentively by asking questions to clarify information.

Vocabulary

- ● What do you see that is yellow?
- ■ What do you see that is purple?
- ▲ What do you see that is orange?

Listening and Speaking

- ● What happens first in the story?
- ■ What happens next in the story?
- ▲ What happens last in the story?

Vocabulary

Color Words

yellow

purple

orange

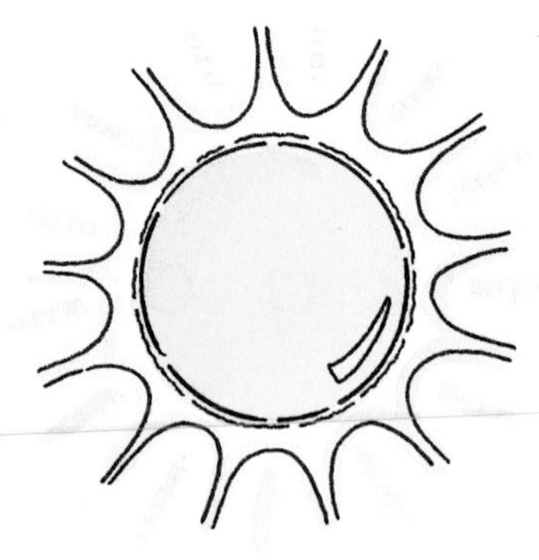

Listening and Speaking

Listen for Sequence

Be a good listener!

TEKS

K.6.B Discuss the big idea (theme) of a well-known fable and connect it to personal experience. **K.6.C.1** Recognize sensory details. **K.8.B.1** Describe characters in a story. **RC-K.F** Make connections to ideas in other texts and discuss textual evidence.

The Ant and the Grasshopper

1

Let's Practice It!

Fable

- ● Listen to the fable.
- ■ How are the two characters different?
- ▲ What is the field like in summer? in winter?
- ★ How is this story like "The Boy Who Cried 'Wolf!'"?
- ♥ What does this fable teach you?

2

TEKS
K.2.D.1 Distinguish orally presented rhyming pairs of words from non-rhyming pairs. K.2.E.1 Recognize spoken alliteration or groups of words that begin with the same onset or initial sound. K.2.H.1 Isolate the initial sound in spoken one-syllable words.
Phonemic Awareness
Let's Listen for
Read Together
Initial Sounds
Say *Sam, Seth, Sue.* What sound do you hear at the beginning of these names?
Point to the sun. Find three things that begin with /s/, like *sun.*
Point to these pictures and say the words: *table, soap, fork.* Do they begin the same? What about *salt, socks, silverware?*
Which words rhyme? socks/clocks? Sam/Sally? Sue/you?
What sounds might you hear in a school lunchroom?
READING STREET ONLINE
BIG QUESTION VIDEO
www.TexasReadingStreet.com

TEKS
K.6.A.1 Identify elements of a story including setting.

Comprehension

Envision It!

Literary Elements

READING STREET ONLINE
PICTURE IT! ANIMATION
www.TexasReadingStreet.com

Characters

Setting

Plot

Phonics

Initial *Ss*

Words I Can Blend

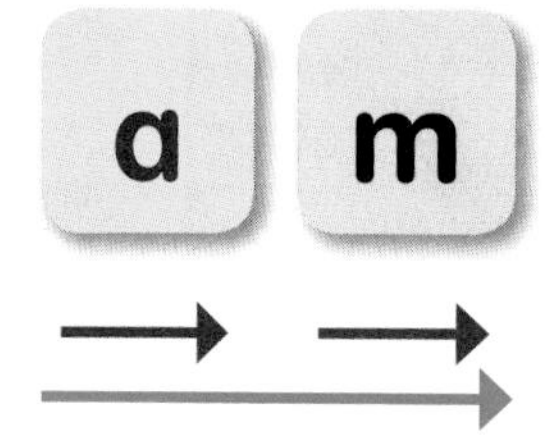

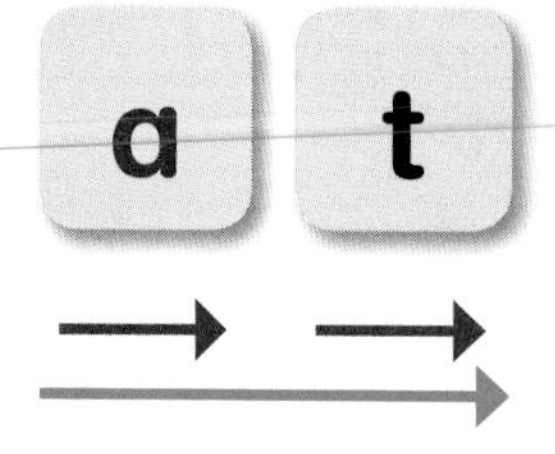

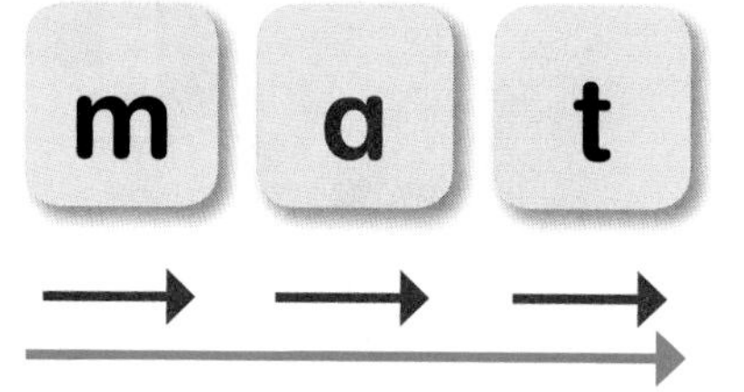

High-Frequency Words

Words I Can Read

have

is

Sentences I Can Read

1. I have Sam.
2. Sam is little.
3. Sam is a .

TEKS
K.3.A.1 Identify the common sounds that letters represent. **K.3.B.1** Use knowledge of letter-sound relationships to decode regular words in text. **K.3.D** Identify and read at least 25 high-frequency words from a commonly used list.

Phonics

I Can Read!

Decodable Reader

- Consonant *Ss*
  Sam
  sat
- High-Frequency Words
  I
  am
  have
  a
  the
  is
- Read the story.

READING STREET ONLINE
DECODABLE eBOOKS
www.TexasReadingStreet.com

Sam and Tam

Written by Paul Thomas
Illustrated by Katie Snell

I am Sam.

I have a mat.

Sam sat at the mat.

I am Tam.

Tam is at the mat.

Tam sat at the mat.

Tam sat.
Sam sat.

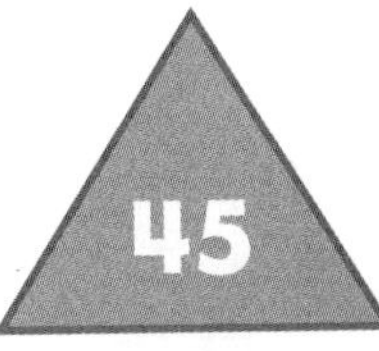

TEKS
K.6.A.1 Identify elements of a story including setting. **K.10.B.1** Retell important facts in a text, heard or read.

Envision It! | Retell

Big Book

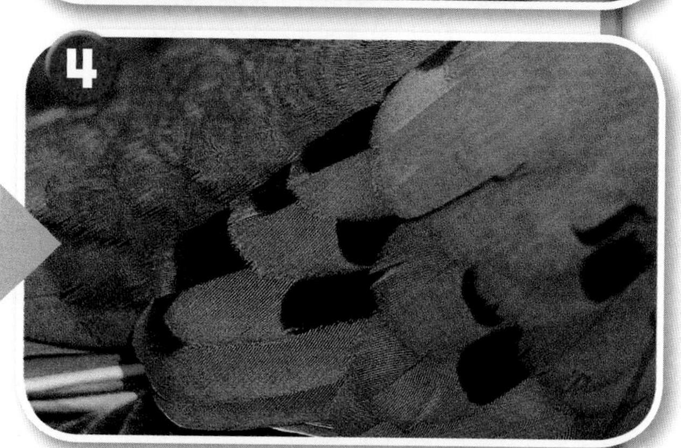

READING STREET ONLINE
RETELL
www.TexasReadingStreet.com

Read Together

Think, Talk, and Write

1. What did you learn about nature from the story?

Text to Self

2. Where does *Nature Spy* take place?

Setting

3. Look back and write.

TEKS
K.21.B.1 Follow oral directions that involve a short related sequence of actions. **K.23.A.1** Follow agreed-upon rules for discussion, including taking turns.

Let's Learn It!

Vocabulary

- Talk about the pictures.
- What grows near your home?

Listening and Speaking

- Follow AlphaBuddy's directions.
- Act like an animal.

Vocabulary

Nature Words

Listening and Speaking

Listen for Directions

TEKS
K.6.A.3 Identify elements of a story including key events. **K.6.D** Recognize recurring phrases and characters in traditional fairy tales from various cultures. **RC-K.A** Discuss the purposes for reading and listening to various texts.

Let's Practice It!

Fairy Tale

- Listen to the fairy tale.
- How can you tell this is a fairy tale?
- Why does the elf grant Josef three wishes?
- How do Josef and Anna waste two wishes?
- Why do people like to read and listen to fairy tales?

3

4

5

TEKS
K.2.B.1 Identify syllables in spoken words. **K.2.E.1** Recognize spoken alliteration or groups of words that begin with the same spoken onset or initial sound. **K.2.H.1** Isolate the initial sound in spoken one-syllable words.

Phonemic Awareness

Let's Listen for

Initial Sounds

Read Together

- Say *Pat, Pam, Pete.* What sound do you hear at the beginning of these names?
- Find three things in the picture that begin like *Pat.*
- Point to these pictures and say the words: *paper, panda, penguin.* Do they begin the same? What about *pig, door, street?*
- Name a color you see in the picture. Clap the words parts. How many claps?

READING STREET ONLINE
BIG QUESTION VIDEO
www.TexasReadingStreet.com

8 9
7
5 6
4
2 3
1

TEKS
K.10.A Identify the topic and details in expository text heard or read, referring to the words and/or illustrations.

Comprehension

Envision It!

Main Idea

READING STREET ONLINE
PICTURE IT! ANIMATION
www.TexasReadingStreet.com

TEKS
K.3.B Use knowledge of letter-sound relationships to decode regular words in text and independent of content. **K.3.D** Identify and read at least 25 high-frequency words from a commonly used list.

READING STREET ONLINE
ALPHABET CARDS
www.TexasReadingStreet.com

Phonics

Initial and Final *Pp*

Words I Can Blend

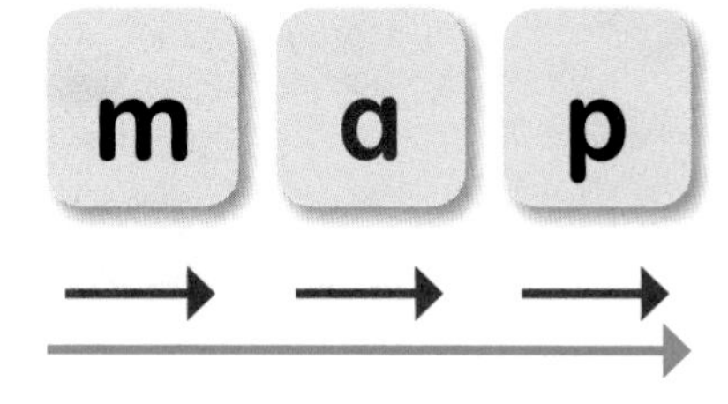

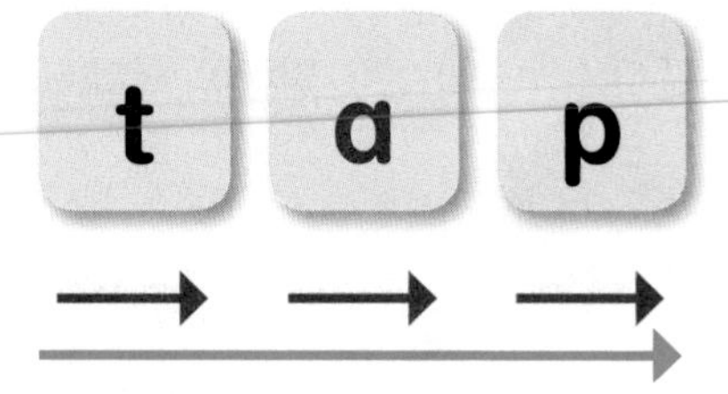

m a t

Words I Can Read

we

my

like

Sentences I Can Read

1. We have a map.
2. We like the map.
3. My map is little.

TEKS
K.3.A.1 Identify the common sounds that letters represent. **K.3.B.1** Use knowledge of letter-sound relationships to decode regular words in text. **K.3.D** Identify and read at least 25 high-frequency words from a commonly used list.

Phonics

I Can Read!

Decodable Reader

- Consonant *Pp*
  Pam
  map
  tap
  pat
- High-Frequency Words

I	am
have	a
the	my
we	like

- Read the story.

READING STREET ONLINE
DECODABLE eBOOKS
www.TexasReadingStreet.com

Decodable Reader 9

My Map

Written by Jerry Moore
Illustrated by Chris Brown

I am Pam.

I have a map.

The map sat at the mat.

I tap my map.

We tap the map.

We pat at the map.

We like the map.

TEKS
K.10.A Identify the topic and details in expository text heard or read, referring to the words and/or illustrations. **K.10.B.1** Retell important events in a text, heard or read. **RC-K.F.3** Make connections to the larger community.

Envision It! Retell

Big Book

READING STREET ONLINE
RETELL
www.TexasReadingStreet.com

Read Together

Think, Talk, and Write

1. How are most animal babies the same? Text to World

2. What is *Animal Babies in Grasslands* about?

Main Idea

3. Look back and write.

TEKS
K.21.A Listen attentively by facing speakers and asking questions to clarify information. **K.23** Follow agreed-upon rules for discussion, including taking turns and speaking one at a time.

Let's Learn It!

Vocabulary

- Talk about the pictures.
- Where do these animal babies live?

Listening and Speaking

- Say one thing about yourself.
- Listen to others talk about themselves.

Vocabulary

Words for Animal Babies

puppy

kitten

chick

calf

Listening and Speaking

Discussion

Be a good speaker!

TEKS
K.4.B Ask and respond to questions about texts read aloud. **K.6.B** Discuss the big idea (theme)of a well-known folk tale and connect it to personal experience. **K.6.D.6** Recognize recurring characters in traditional folk tales from various cultures.

Anansi's Hat Shaking Dance

Let's Practice It!

Folk Tale

- ● Listen to the folk tale.
- ■ Where and when does the story take place?
- ▲ Why does Anansi put his hat back on?
- ★ Tell about Anansi. What is he like?
- ♥ What do you learn from Anansi that can help you?
- ✱ What questions do you have about this folk tale?

1

2

3

4

TEKS
K.2.B.1 Identify syllables in spoken words. **K.2.E.1** Recognize spoken alliteration or groups of words that begin with the same spoken onset or initial sound. **K.2.H.1** Isolate the initial sound in spoken one-syllable words.

Let's Listen for

Initial Sounds

Read Together

- ● Say *Carl, Cam, Cate.* What sound do you hear at the beginning of these names?
- ■ Point to the cart in the picture. Find three things that begin with /k/, like *cart.*
- ▲ Name other words that begin with /k/.
- ★ Point to and say, *Carrots and cucumbers are in the cart.* What sound do you hear repeated?
- ♥ Say *cucumber.* Clap the word parts. How many claps?

READING STREET ONLINE
BIG QUESTION VIDEO
www.TexasReadingStreet.com

TEKS

★ Determine whether a story is real or make-believe and tell why.

Comprehension

Envision It!

Realism and Fantasy

READING STREET ONLINE
PICTURE IT! ANIMATION
www.TexasReadingStreet.com

4+4
2+3
1+2
=
?
3
8
5
3

TEKS
K.3.C Recognize that new words are created when letters are changed, added, or deleted. **K.3.D** Identify and read at least 25 high-frequency words from a commonly used list. **Also K.3.B.**

Envision It! | Sounds to Know

Cc

cactus

READING STREET ONLINE
ALPHABET CARDS
www.TexasReadingStreet.com

Phonics

Initial and Final *Cc*

Words I Can Blend

High-Frequency Words

Words I Can Read

we

my

like

Sentences I Can Read

1. I like Cam.
2. We like to sit.
3. We like my cat.

TEKS
K.3.A.1 Identify the common sounds that letters represent. **K.3.B.1** Use knowledge of letter-sound relationships to decode regular words in text. **K.3.D** Identify and read at least 25 high-frequency words from a commonly used list.

Phonics

I Can Read!

Decodable Reader

- Consonant *Cc*
  Cam
  Mac
  cap
- High-Frequency Words
  I, am, we, have, a, is, the, my, like
- Read the story.

READING STREET ONLINE
DECODABLE eBOOKS
www.TexasReadingStreet.com

Decodable Reader 10

My Cap

Written by Sue Bear
Illustrated by Lori Burk

I am Cam.
I am Mac.

We have a cap.

Cam is at the cap.

Is the cap my cap?

Mac is at the cap.

Is the cap my cap?

I like my cap.

TEKS

K.8.A.1 Retell a main event from a story read aloud. **RC-K.E.1** Retell important events in stories.
★ Determine whether a story is real or make-believe and tell why.

Envision It! | Retell

Big Book

READING STREET ONLINE
RETELL
www.TexasReadingStreet.com

Think, Talk, and Write

Read Together

1. What does a bear do in the winter? **Text to World**

2. Which story is about real animals? Which is about make-believe animals?

Realism and Fantasy

3. Look back and write.

K.21.A Listen attentively by facing speakers and asking questions to clarify information. **K.23** Follow agreed-upon rules for discussion, including taking turns and speaking one at a time.

Let's

It!

Vocabulary

- Talk about the pictures.
- Which season is your favorite?

Listening and Speaking

- Where do AlphaBuddy's stories take place?

Vocabulary

Words for Nature

spring

summer

fall

Listening and Speaking

Listen for Setting

TEKS
K.6.D.5 Recognize recurring characters in traditional lullabies from various cultures. **K.7.A** Respond to rhythm and rhyme in poetry through identifying a regular beat and similarities in word sounds.

Rock-a-Bye, Baby

1

Let's Practice It!

Lullaby

- ● Listen to the lullaby.
- ■ Sing the lullaby. Sway in time to its rhythm.
- ▲ Which words in the lullaby rhyme?
- ★ Who is often a main character in a lullaby? Why?
- ♥ Which part of the lullaby is make-believe?

2

TEKS
K.2.B.1 Identify syllables in spoken words. **K.2.E.1** Recognize spoken alliteration or groups of words that begin with the same spoken onset or initial sound.

Phonemic Awareness

Let's Listen for

Initial Sounds

Read Together

- Say *Isabel, Izzy, Inga.* What sound do you hear at the beginning of these names?
- Find three things that begin with /i/, like *Isabel.*
- Point to these pictures: *ink, iguana, igloo.* Do they begin the same? What about *insects, books, posters?*
- Say *inventor.* Clap the word parts. How many claps?
- What sounds would you hear in a library? What kind of voice should you use?

READING STREET ONLINE
BIG QUESTION VIDEO
www.TexasReadingStreet.com

TEKS

★ Describe the events of a story in order.

Comprehension

Envision It!

Sequence

READING STREET ONLINE
PICTURE IT! ANIMATION
www.TexasReadingStreet.com

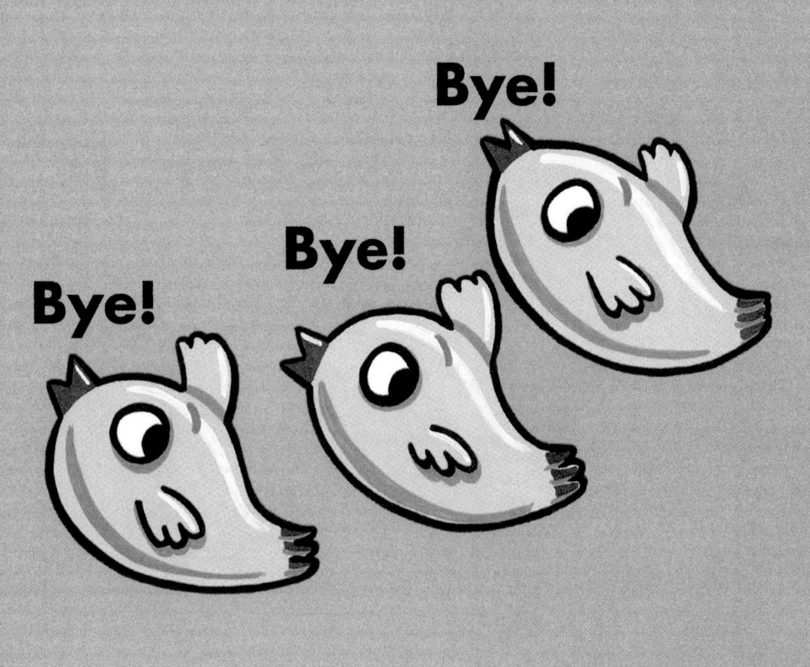
Bye!
Bye!
Bye!

TEKS
K.3.C Recognize that new words are created when letters are changed, added, or deleted. **K.3.D** Identify and read at least 25 high-frequency words from a commonly used list. **Also K.3.B.**

Envision It! Sounds to Know

Ii

Igloo

READING STREET ONLINE
ALPHABET CARDS
www.TexasReadingStreet.com

Phonics

Short *Ii*

Words I Can Blend

s i t

T i m

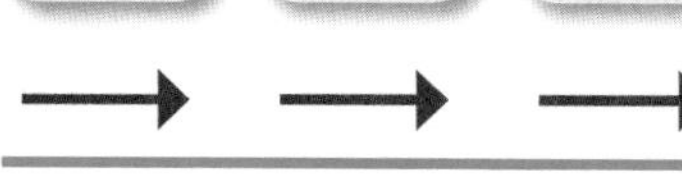

t i p

p i t

s i p

Words I Can Read

he

for

Sentences I Can Read

1. He is a cat.
2. The cat is for Tim.
3. He can sit for Tim.

TEKS
K.3.A.1 Identify the common sounds that letters represent. **K.3.B.1** Use knowledge of letter-sound relationships to decode regular words in text. **K.3.D** Identify and read at least 25 high-frequency words from a commonly used list.

Phonics

I Can Read!

Decodable Reader

- Short *i*
  Tip
  it
  sit
- High-Frequency Words
  is
  a
  he
  my
  for
- Read the story.

READING STREET ONLINE
DECODABLE eBOOKS
www.TexasReadingStreet.com

Tip and Pat

Decodable Reader 11

Written by Kate Brand
Illustrated by Carl Johnson

Tip is a cat.

He is my cat.

Pat is a cat.

He is my cat.

It is for Tip.

It is for Pat.

Sit, Tip, sit.
Sit, Pat, sit.

TEKS

K.10.B.1 Retell important events in a text, heard or read. **RC-K.F.2** Make connections to ideas in other texts. ★ Describe the events of a story in order.

Envision It! | Retell

Big Book

1

2

3

4

5

6

READING STREET ONLINE
RETELL
www.TexasReadingStreet.com

Think, Talk, and Write

Read Together

1. Which bed reminded you of *Bear Snores On*? Text to Text

2. Where does the dormouse go first in the story? Where does she go last?

Sequence

3. Look back and write.

TEKS
K.5.A Identify and use words that name sequences. **K.22** Share information and ideas by speaking audibly and clearly using the conventions of language.

Let's Learn It!

Vocabulary

- Talk about the pictures.
- What do you do to get ready for school? Use sequence words.

Listening and Speaking

- What do the clocks look like?
- What do the dogs look like?

Vocabulary

Sequence Words

first

second

next

last

Listening and Speaking

Give a Description

Be a good speaker!

TEKS
K.7.A.1 Respond to rhythm in poetry through identifying a regular beat. **RC-K.D.3** Make inferences based on the illustrations. **RC-K.F** Make connections to own experiences and discuss textual evidence.

The House That Jack Built

Let's Practice It!

Nursery Rhyme

- ● Listen to the rhyme.
- ■ Recite the rhyme. Clap your hands to show the beats.
- ▲ How does Jack feel about his house? How can you tell?
- ★ Tell about a time when it rained on you. Did you feel like these animals felt?

4

5

6

TEKS
K.2.H.1 Isolate the initial sound in spoken one-syllable words.

Phonemic Awareness

Let's Listen for

Initial Sounds

Read Together

- Say the sound you hear at the beginning of *in, ask, sign, pears, cast.*
- Point to the picture of *in*. Find a picture that begins with /i/, with /a/, with /s/, with /p/, with /k/.
- Name other words that begin with /i/, /a/, /s/, /p/, /k/.

READING STREET ONLINE
BIG QUESTION VIDEO
www.TexasReadingStreet.com

TEKS

★ Determine whether a story is real or make-believe and tell why.

Comprehension

Envision It!

Realism and Fantasy

READING STREET ONLINE
PICTURE IT! ANIMATION
www.TexasReadingStreet.com

4+4
2+3
1+2
=
?
3
8 5 3

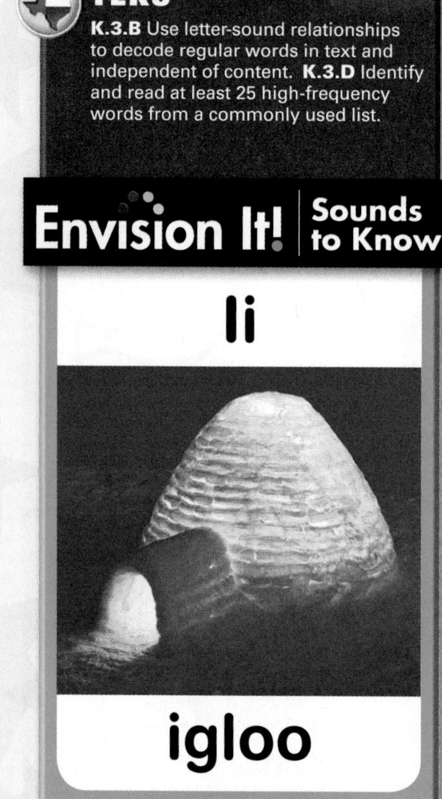

Phonics

Short *Ii*

Words I Can Blend

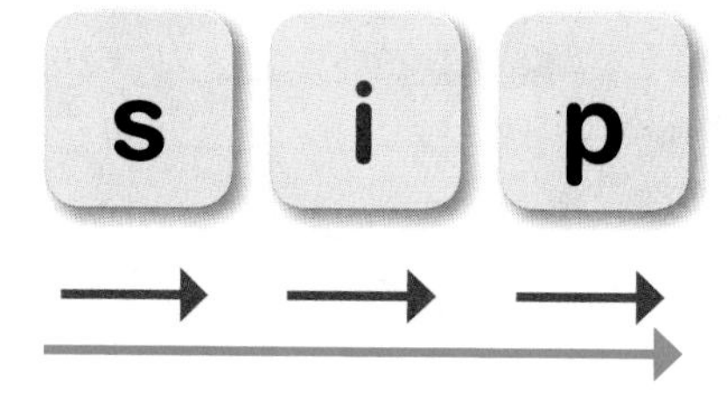

i t

p i t

High-Frequency Words

Words I Can Read

he

for

Sentences I Can Read

1. He is my cat, Pip.
2. Pip can sit for Tim.
3. He can tap it.

TEKS
K.3.A.1 Identify the common sounds that letters represent. **K.3.B.1** Use knowledge of letter-sound relationships to decode regular words in text. **K.3.D** Identify and read at least 25 high-frequency words from a commonly used list.

Phonics

I Can Read!

Decodable Reader

- Short *i*
  sit
  Tim
  tip
  it
- High-Frequency Words

I	am
have	he
is	my
we	a
for	

- Read the story.

READING STREET ONLINE
DECODABLE eBOOKS
www.TexasReadingStreet.com

Decodable Reader 12

Tim and Sam

Written by Joei Shavitz
Illustrated by Lawrence Paul

I am Sam.
I sit.

Tim sat.
I have Tim.

He is my cat.

I pat Tim.

We tip.

I am Sam.
I sit.

It is a mat for Tim.

TEKS
K.8.A.1 Retell a main event from a story read aloud. **RC-K.E.1** Retell important events in stories. **RC-K.F.2** Make connections to ideas in other texts. ★ Determine whether a story is real or make-believe and tell why.

Envision It! | Retell

Big Book

READING STREET ONLINE
RETELL
www.TexasReadingStreet.com

Think, Talk, and Write

1. How are the plants in *Flowers* and *Jack and the Beanstalk* the same? How are they different? **Text to Text**

2. Which story is real?

Which is make-believe?

Realism and Fantasy

3. Look back and write.

TEKS
K.5.A Identify and use words that name directions. **K.22** Share information and ideas by speaking audibly and clearly using conventions of language. **K.23.A.1** Follow agreed-upon rules for discussion, including taking turns.

Let's Learn It!

Vocabulary

- Talk about the picture.
- Raise you right hand.
- Raise your left hand.

Listening and Speaking

- What happens in the story?

Vocabulary

Direction Words

left right

Listening and Speaking

Listen for Plot

TEKS
K.10.A Identify the topic and details in expository text heard or read, referring to the words and/or illustrations. K.10.C.1 Discuss the way authors group information in text. K.10.D Use titles and illustrations to make predictions about text.
Let's Practice It!
Expository Text
Look at the title and the pictures. What will the selection be about?
Listen to the selection.
How do roots help a plant?
Where are the leaves on a plant?
What does the author tell about first? second? third? last?
Parts of a Plant
Leaf
Roots

Flower
Stem

Words for Things That Go

airplane

bike

truck

car

bus

van

boat

train

Words for Colors

Words for Shapes

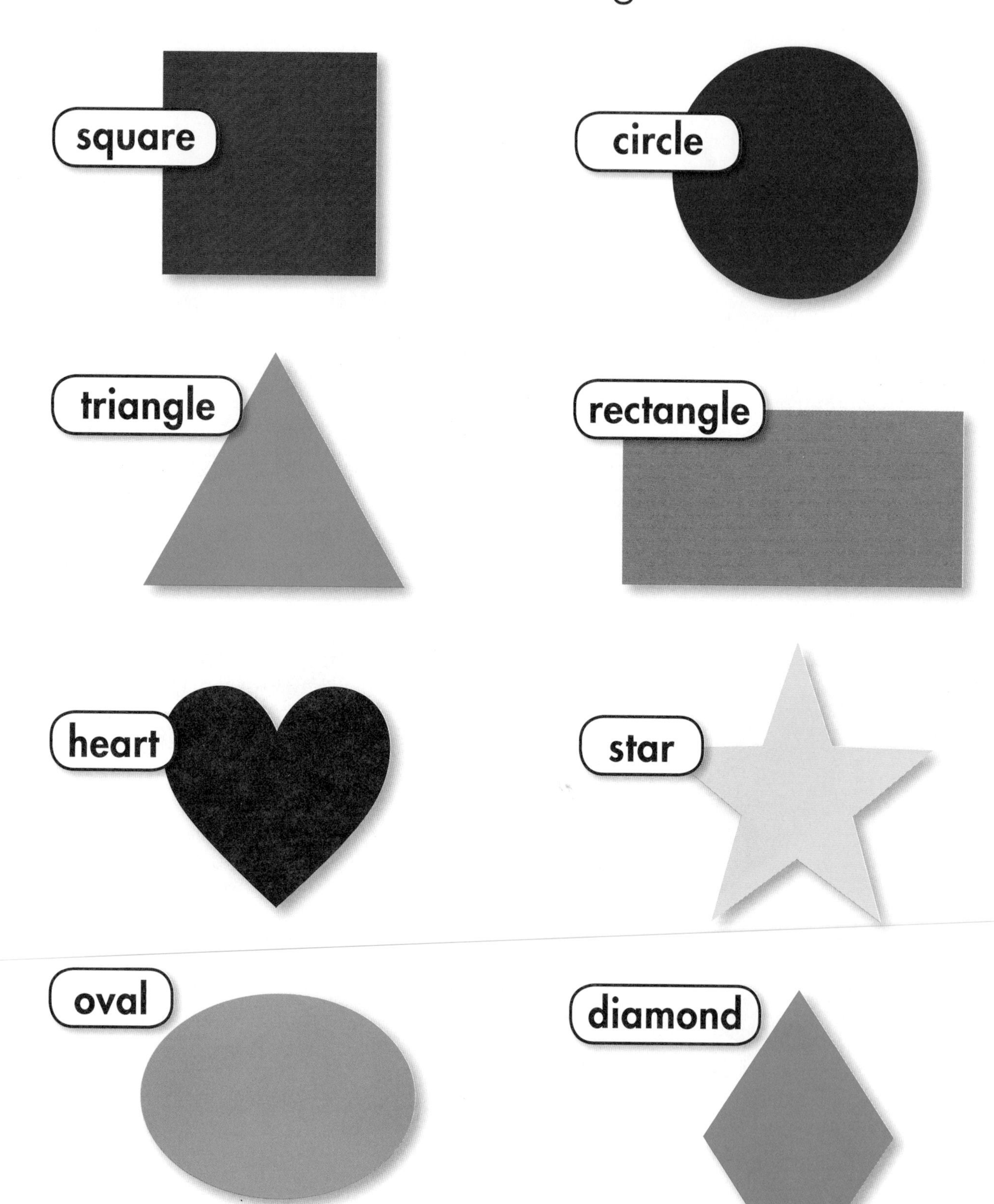

Words for Places

school

home

park

train station

police station

fire station

post office

library

Words for Animals

fish
whale
butterfly
bear
panda
caterpillar
calf
cow
beaver

Words for Actions

Position Words

My Classroom

bookcase

easel

books

desk

markers

crayons

pencil

teacher

toys

paper

chair

blocks

table

rug

Words for Feelings

happy

frightened

worried

excited

angry

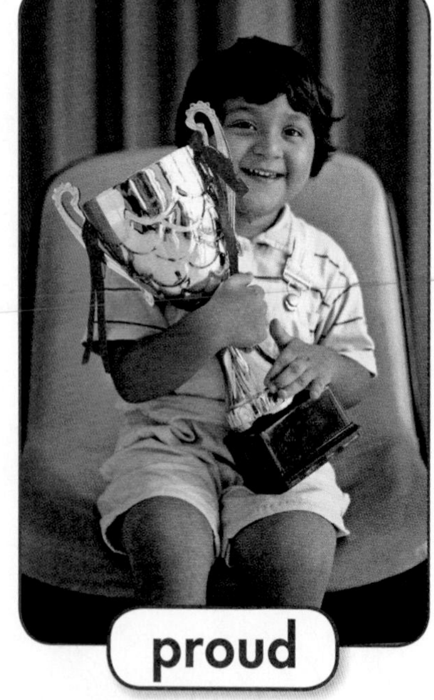
proud

sad

surprised

My Family

mom
mother
dad
father
sister
grandmother
grandfather
brother

Illustrations

Cover: Rob Hefferan

12 Natalia Vasquez

28, 32, 48, 69, 88–89, 108–109 Mick Reid

30–31 Paul Meisel

50–51 Colleen Madden

52 Carolyn Croll

59–65 Maria Mola

70–71 Carolina Farias

72 Susan Mitchell

79–85 Wednesday Kirwan

90–91 David Austin Clar

92 Anthony Lewis

99–105 Cale Atkinson

110–111 Remy Simard

112 Jannie Ho

119–125 Robbie Short.

Photographs

Every effort has been made to secure permission and provide appropriate credit for photographic material. The publisher deeply regrets any omission and pledges to correct errors called to its attention in subsequent editions.

Unless otherwise acknowledged, all photographs are the property of Pearson Education, Inc.

Photo locators denoted as follows: Top (T), Center (C), Bottom (B), Left (L), Right (R), Background (Bkgd)

10 (B) ©William Leaman/Alamy

49 Cyril Laubscher/©DK Images, Dave King/©DK Images, Geoff Brightling/©DK Images, Mike Dunning/©DK Images

68 ©DK Images, Jane Burton/©DK Images

130 (T) ©DK Images

131 (T, B) ©DK Images.